Mutual Funds

A Guide for Investors

OFFICE *of* INVESTOR
EDUCATION *and* ADVOCACY

Information is an investor's best tool

Mutual Funds

Over the past decade, American investors increasingly have turned to mutual funds to save for retirement and other financial goals. Mutual funds can offer the advantages of diversification and professional management. But, as with other investment choices, investing in mutual funds involves risk. And fees and taxes will diminish a fund's returns. It pays to understand both the upsides and downsides of mutual fund investing and how to choose products that match your goals and tolerance for risk.

This brochure explains the basics of mutual fund investing, how mutual funds work, what factors to consider before investing, and how to avoid common pitfalls.

U.S. Securities and Exchange Commission
Office of Investor Education and Advocacy
100 F Street, NE
Washington, DC 20549-0213
Toll-free: (800) 732-0330
Website: www.investor.gov

Table of Contents

Key Points to Remember

☑ Mutual funds are *not* guaranteed or insured by the FDIC or any other government agency—even if you buy through a bank and the fund carries the bank's name. You can lose money investing in mutual funds.

☑ Past performance is not a reliable indicator of future performance so don't be dazzled by last year's high returns. But past performance can help you assess a fund's volatility over time.

☑ All mutual funds have costs that lower your investment returns. Shop around and compare fees.

How Mutual Funds Work

WHAT THEY ARE

A mutual fund is a company that pools money from many investors and invests the money in stocks, bonds, short-term money-market instruments, other securities or assets, or some combination of these investments. The combined holdings the mutual fund owns are known as its portfolio. Each share represents an investor's proportionate ownership of the fund's holdings and the income those holdings generate.

OTHER TYPES OF INVESTMENT COMPANIES

Legally known as an "open-end company," a mutual fund is one of three basic types of investment companies. While this brochure discusses only mutual funds, you should be aware that other pooled investment vehicles exist and may offer features that you desire. The two other basic types of investment companies are:

- **Closed-end funds**—which, unlike mutual funds, sell a fixed number of shares at one time (in an initial public offering) that later trade on a secondary market; and

- **Unit Investment Trusts (UITs)**—which make a one-time public offering of only a specific, fixed number of redeemable securities called "units" and which will terminate and dissolve on a date specified at the creation of the UIT.

"Exchange-traded funds" (ETFs) are a type of investment company that aims to achieve the same return as a particular market index. They can be either open-end companies or UITs. But ETFs are not considered to be, and are not permitted to call themselves, mutual funds.

CHARACTERISTICS OF FUNDS

Some of the traditional, distinguishing characteristics of mutual funds include the following:

➣ Investors purchase mutual fund shares from the fund itself (or through a broker for the fund) instead of from other investors on a secondary market, such as the New York Stock Exchange or Nasdaq Stock Market.

➣ The price that investors pay for mutual fund shares is the fund's per share net asset value (NAV) plus any shareholder fees that the fund imposes at the time of purchase (such as sales loads).

➤ Mutual fund shares are "redeemable," meaning investors can sell their shares back to the fund (or to a broker acting for the fund).

➤ Mutual funds generally create and sell new shares to accommodate new investors. In other words, it sells its shares on a continuous basis, although some funds stop selling when, for example, they become too large.

➤ The investment portfolios of mutual funds typically are managed by separate entities known as "investment advisers" that are registered with the SEC.

ADVANTAGES AND DISADVANTAGES

Every investment has advantages and disadvantages. But it's important to remember that features that matter to one investor may not be important to you. Whether any particular feature is an advantage for you will depend on your unique circumstances. For some investors, mutual funds provide an attractive investment choice because they generally offer the following features:

- **Professional Management**—Professional money managers research, select, and monitor the performance of the securities the fund purchases.

- **Diversification**—Diversification is an investing strategy that can be neatly summed up as "Don't put all your eggs in one basket." Spreading your investments across a wide range of companies and industry sectors can help lower your risk if a company or sector fails. Some investors find it easier to achieve diversification through ownership of mutual funds rather than through ownership of individual stocks or bonds.

- **Affordability**—Some mutual funds accommodate investors who don't have a lot of money to invest by setting relatively low dollar amounts for initial purchases, subsequent monthly purchases, or both.

- **Liquidity**—Mutual fund investors can readily redeem their shares at the current NAV—plus any fees and charges assessed on redemption—at any time.

But mutual funds also have features that some investors might view as disadvantages, such as:

- **Costs Despite Negative Returns**—Investors must pay sales charges, annual fees, and other expenses (which we discuss in detail on page 13) regardless of how the fund performs. And, depending on the timing of their investment, investors may also have to pay taxes on any capital gains distribution they receive—even if the fund went on to perform poorly after they bought shares.

- **Lack of Control**—Investors typically cannot ascertain the exact make-up of a fund's portfolio at any given time, nor can they directly influence which securities the fund manager buys and sells or the timing of those trades.

- **Price Uncertainty**—With an individual stock, you can obtain real-time (or close to real-time) pricing information with relative ease by checking financial websites or by calling your broker. You can also monitor how a stock's price changes from hour to hour—or even second to second. By contrast, with a mutual fund, the price at which you purchase or redeem shares will typically depend on the fund's NAV, which the fund might not calculate until many hours after you've placed your order. In general, mutual funds must calculate their NAV at least once every business day, typically after the major U.S. exchanges close.

DIFFERENT TYPES OF FUNDS

When it comes to investing in mutual funds, investors have literally thousands of choices. Before you invest in any given fund, decide whether the investment strategy and risks of the fund are a good fit for you. The first step to successful investing is figuring out your financial goals and risk tolerance—either on your own or with the help of a financial professional. Once you know what you're saving for, when you'll need the money, and how much risk you can tolerate, you can more easily narrow your choices.

Most mutual funds fall into one of three main categories—money market funds, bond funds (also called "fixed income" funds), and stock funds (also called "equity" funds). Each type has different features and different risks and rewards. Generally, the higher the potential return, the higher the risk of loss.

Money Market Funds

Money market funds have relatively low risks, compared to other mutual funds (and most other investments). By law, they can invest in only certain high-quality, short-term investments issued by the U.S. Government, U.S. corporations, and state and local governments. Money market funds try to keep their net asset value (NAV)—which represents the value of one share in a fund—at a stable $1.00 per share. But the NAV may fall below $1.00 if the fund's investments perform poorly. Investor losses have been rare, but they are possible.

Money market funds pay dividends that generally reflect short-term interest rates, and historically the returns for money market funds have been lower than for either bond or stock funds. That's why "inflation risk"—the risk that inflation will outpace and erode investment returns over time—can be a potential concern for investors in money market funds.

Bond Funds

Bond funds generally have higher risks than money market funds, largely because they typically pursue strategies aimed at producing higher yields. Unlike money market funds, the SEC's rules do not restrict bond funds to high-quality or short-term investments. Because there are many different types of bonds, bond funds can vary dramatically in their risks and rewards. Some of the risks associated with bond funds include:

Credit Risk—the possibility that companies or other issuers whose bonds are owned by the fund may fail to pay their debts (including the debt owed to holders of their bonds). Credit risk is less of a factor for bond funds that invest in insured bonds or U.S. Treasury Bonds. By contrast, those that invest in the bonds of companies with poor credit ratings generally will be subject to higher risk.

Interest Rate Risk—the risk that the market value of the bonds will go down when interest rates go up. Because of this, you can lose money in any bond fund, including those that invest only in insured bonds or U.S. Treasury Bonds. Funds that invest in longer-term bonds tend to have higher interest rate risk.

Prepayment Risk—the chance that a bond will be paid off early. For example, if interest rates fall, a bond issuer may decide to pay off (or "retire") its debt and issue new bonds that pay a lower rate. When this happens, the fund may not be able to reinvest the proceeds in an investment with as high a return or yield.

Stock Funds

Although a stock fund's value can rise and fall quickly (and dramatically) over the short term, historically stocks have performed better over the long term than other types of investments—including corporate bonds, government bonds, and treasury securities.

Overall "market risk" poses the greatest potential danger for investors in stocks funds. Stock prices can fluctuate for a broad range of reasons—such as the overall strength of the economy or demand for particular products or services.

Not all stock funds are the same. For example:

* *Growth* funds focus on stocks that may not pay a regular dividend but have the potential for large capital gains.

* *Income* funds invest in stocks that pay regular dividends.

* *Index* funds aim to achieve the same return as a particular market index, such as the S&P 500 Composite Stock Price Index, by investing in all—or perhaps a representative sample—of the companies included in an index.

* *Sector* funds may specialize in a particular industry segment, such as technology or consumer products stocks.

HOW TO BUY AND SELL SHARES

You can purchase shares in some mutual funds by contacting the fund directly. Other mutual fund shares are sold mainly through brokers, banks, financial planners, or insurance agents. All mutual funds will redeem (buy back) your shares on any business day and must send you the payment within seven days.

A "family of funds" is a group of mutual funds that share administrative and distribution systems. Each fund in a family may have different investment objectives and follow different strategies.

Some funds offer exchange privileges within a family of funds, allowing shareholders to transfer their holdings from one fund to another as their investment goals or tolerance for risk change. While some funds impose fees for exchanges, most funds typically do not. To learn more about a funds exchange policies, call the fund's toll-free number, visit its website, or read the "shareholder information" section of the prospectus.

Bear in mind that exchanges have tax consequences. Even if the fund doesn't charge you for the transfer, you'll be liable for any capital gain on the sale of your old shares or, depending on the circumstances, eligible to take a capital loss. We'll discuss taxes in further detail below.

The easiest way to determine the value of your shares is to call the fund's toll-free number or visit its website. The financial pages of major newspapers sometimes print the NAVs for various mutual funds. When you buy shares, you pay the current NAV per share plus any fee the fund assesses at the time of purchase, such as a purchase sales load or other type of purchase fee. When you sell your shares, the fund will pay you the NAV minus any fee the fund assesses at the time of redemption, such as a deferred (or back-end) sales load or redemption fee. A fund's NAV goes up or down daily as its holdings change in value.

HOW FUNDS CAN EARN MONEY FOR YOU

You can earn money from your investment in three ways:

1. **Dividend Payments**—A fund may earn income in the form of dividends and interest on the securities in its portfolio. The fund then pays its shareholders nearly all of the income (minus disclosed expenses) it has earned in the form of dividends.

2. **Capital Gains Distributions**—The price of the securities a fund owns may increase. When a fund sells a security that has increased in price, the fund has a capital gain. At the end of the year, most funds distribute these capital gains (minus any capital losses) to investors.

3. **Increased NAV**—If the market value of a fund's portfolio increases, after deduction of expenses and liabilities, then the value (NAV) of the fund and its shares increases. The higher NAV reflects the higher value of your investment.

With respect to dividend payments and capital gains distributions, funds usually will give you a choice: the fund can send you a check or other form of payment, or you can have your dividends or distributions *reinvested* in the fund to buy more shares (often without paying an additional sales load).

Factors to Consider

Thinking about your long-term investment strategies and tolerance for risk can help you decide what type of fund is best suited for you. But you should also consider the effect that fees and taxes will have on your returns over time.

DEGREES OF RISK

All funds carry some level of risk. You may lose some or all of the money you invest—your principal—because the securities held by a fund go up and down in value. Dividend or interest payments may also fluctuate as market conditions change.

Before you invest, be sure to read a fund's prospectus and shareholder reports to learn about its investment strategy and the potential risks. Funds with higher rates of return may take risks that are beyond your comfort level and are inconsistent with your financial goals.

A WORD ABOUT DERIVATIVES

Derivatives are financial instruments whose performance is derived, at least in part, from the performance of an underlying asset, security, or index. Even small market movements can dramatically affect their value, sometimes in unpredictable ways.

There are many types of derivatives with many different uses. A fund's prospectus will disclose whether and how it may use derivatives. You may also want to call a fund and ask how it uses these instruments.

FEES AND EXPENSES

As with any business, running a mutual fund involves costs—including shareholder transaction costs, investment advisory fees, and marketing and distribution expenses. Funds pass along these costs to investors by imposing fees and expenses. It is important that you understand these charges because they lower your returns.

Some funds impose "shareholder fees" directly on investors whenever they buy or sell shares. In addition, every fund has regular, recurring, fund-wide "operating expenses." Funds typically pay their operating expenses out of fund assets—which means that investors indirectly pay these costs.

SEC rules require funds to disclose both shareholder fees and operating expenses in a "fee table" near the front of a fund's prospectus. The lists below will help you decode the fee table and understand the various fees a fund may impose:

Shareholder Fees

* **Sales Charge (Load) on Purchases**—the amount you pay when you buy shares in a mutual fund. Also known as a "front-end load," this fee typically goes to the brokers that sell the fund's shares. Front-end loads reduce the amount of your investment. For example, let's say you have $1,000 and want to invest it in a mutual fund with a 5% front-end load. The $50 sales load you must pay comes off the top, and the remaining $950 will be invested in the fund. According to the rules of FINRA, a front-end load cannot be higher than 8.5% of your investment.

* **Purchase Fee**—another type of fee that some funds charge their shareholders when they buy shares. Unlike a front-end sales load, an after purchase fee is paid to the fund (not to a broker) and is typically imposed to defray some of the fund's costs associated with the purchase.

* **Deferred Sales Charge (Load)**—a fee you pay when you sell your shares. Also known as a "back-end load," this fee typically goes to the brokers that sell the fund's shares. The most common type of back-end sales load is the "contingent deferred sales load" (also known as a "CDSC" or "CDSL"). The amount of this type of load will depend on how long the investor holds his or her shares and typically decreases to zero if the investor holds his or her shares long enough.

* **Redemption Fee**—another type of fee that some funds charge their shareholders when they sell or redeem shares. Unlike a deferred sales load, a redemption fee is paid to the fund (not to a broker) and is typically used to defray fund costs associated with a shareholder's redemption.

- **Exchange Fee**—a fee that some funds impose on shareholders if they exchange (transfer) to another fund within the same fund group or "family of funds."

- **Account Fee**—a fee that some funds separately impose on investors in connection with the maintenance of their accounts. For example, some funds impose an account maintenance fee on accounts whose value is less than a certain dollar amount.

Annual Fund Operating Expenses

- **Management Fees**—fees that are paid out of fund assets to the fund's investment adviser for investment portfolio management, any other management fees payable to the fund's investment adviser or its affiliates, and administrative fees payable to the investment adviser that are not included in the "Other Expenses" category (discussed below).

- **Distribution [and/or Service] Fees ("12b-1" Fees)**—fees paid by the fund out of fund assets to cover the costs of marketing and selling fund shares and sometimes to cover the costs of providing shareholder services. "Distribution fees" include fees to compensate brokers and others who sell fund shares and to pay for advertising, the printing and mailing of prospectuses to new investors, and the printing and mailing of sales literature. "Shareholder Service Fees" are fees paid to persons to respond to investor inquiries and provide investors with information about their investments.

- **Other Expenses**—expenses not included under "Management Fees" or "Distribution or Service (12b-1) Fees," such as any shareholder service expenses that are not already included in the 12b-1 fees, custodial expenses, legal and accounting expenses, transfer agent expenses, and other administrative expenses.

- **Total Annual Fund Operating Expenses ("Expense Ratio")**—the line of the fee table that represents the total of all of a fund's annual fund operating expenses, expressed as a percentage of the fund's average net assets. Looking at the expense ratio can help you make comparisons among funds.

Be sure to review carefully the fee tables of any funds you're considering, including no-load funds. Even small differences in fees can translate into large differences in returns over time. For example, if you invested $10,000 in a fund that produced a 10% annual return before expenses and had annual operating expenses of 1.5%, then after 20 years you would have roughly $49,725. But if the fund had expenses of only 0.5%, then you would end up with $60,858—an 18% difference.

A WORD ABOUT "NO-LOAD" FUNDS

Some funds call themselves "no-load." As the name implies, this means that the fund does not charge any type of sales load. But, as discussed above, not every type of shareholder fee is a "sales load." A no-load fund may charge fees that are not sales loads, such as purchase fees, redemption fees, exchange fees, and account fees. No-load funds will also have operating expenses.

Some mutual funds that charge front-end sales loads will charge lower sales loads for larger investments. The investment levels required to obtain a reduced sales load are commonly referred to as "breakpoints."

The SEC does not require a fund to offer breakpoints in the fund's sales load. But, if breakpoints exist, the fund must disclose them. In addition, a brokerage firm that is a member of FINRA (formerly known as the National Association of Securities Dealers) should not sell you shares of a fund in an amount that is "just below" the fund's sales load breakpoint simply to earn a higher commission.

Each fund company establishes its own formula for how it will calculate whether an investor is entitled to receive a breakpoint. For that reason, it is important to seek out breakpoint information from your financial advisor or the fund itself. You'll need to ask how a particular fund establishes eligibility for breakpoint discounts, as well as what the fund's breakpoint amounts are.

CLASSES OF FUNDS

Many mutual funds offer more than one class of shares. For example, you may have seen a fund that offers "Class A" and "Class B" shares. Each class will invest in the same "pool" (or investment portfolio) of securities and will have the same investment objectives and policies. But each class will have different shareholder services and/or distribution arrangements with different fees and expenses. As a result, each class will likely have different performance results.

A multi-class structure offers investors the ability to select a fee and expense structure that is most appropriate for their investment goals (including the time that they expect to remain invested in the fund). Here are some key characteristics of the most common mutual fund share classes offered to individual investors:

- **Class A Shares**—Class A shares typically impose a front-end sales load. They also tend to have a lower 12b-1 fee and lower annual expenses than other mutual fund share classes. Be aware that some mutual funds reduce the front-end load as the size of your investment increases. If you're considering Class A shares, be sure to inquire about breakpoints.

- **Class B Shares**—Class B shares typically do not have a front-end sales load. Instead, they may impose a contingent deferred sales load and a 12b-1 fee (along with other annual expenses). Class B shares also might convert automatically to a class with a lower 12b-1 fee if the investor holds the shares long enough.

- **Class C Shares**—Class C shares might have a 12b-1 fee, other annual expenses, and either a front-end or back-end sales load. But the front-end or back-end load for Class C shares tends to be lower than for Class A or Class B shares, respectively. Unlike Class B shares, Class C shares generally do not convert to another class. Class C shares tend to have higher annual expenses than either Class A or Class B shares.

TAX CONSEQUENCES

When you buy and hold an individual stock or bond, you must pay **income tax** each year on the dividends or interest you receive. But you won't have to pay any **capital gains tax** until you actually sell and unless you make a profit.

Mutual funds are different. When you buy and hold mutual fund shares, you will owe income tax on any ordinary dividends in the year you receive or reinvest them. And, in addition to owing taxes on any *personal capital gains* when you sell your shares, you may also have to pay taxes each year on the *fund's capital gains*. That's because the law requires mutual funds to distribute capital gains to shareholders if they sell securities for a profit that can't be offset by a loss.

TAX EXEMPT FUNDS

If you invest in a tax-exempt fund—such as a municipal bond fund—some or all of your dividends will be exempt from federal (and sometimes state and local) income tax. You will, however, owe taxes on any capital gains.

Bear in mind that if you receive a capital gains distribution, you will likely owe taxes—even if the fund has had a negative return from the point during the year when you purchased your shares. For this reason, you should call the fund to find out when it makes distributions so you won't pay more than your fair share of taxes. Some funds post that information on their websites.

SEC rules require mutual funds to disclose in their prospectuses after-tax returns. In calculating after-tax returns, mutual funds must use standardized formulas similar to the ones used to calculate before-tax average annual total returns. You'll find a fund's after-tax returns in the "Risk/Return Summary" section of the prospectus. When comparing funds, be sure to take taxes into account.

Avoiding Common Pitfalls

If you decide to invest in mutual funds, be sure to obtain as much relevant information as possible about the fund *before* you invest. And don't make assumptions about the soundness of the fund based solely on its past performance or its name.

SOURCES OF INFORMATION

Prospectus

When you purchase shares of a mutual fund, the fund *must* provide you with a prospectus. But you can and should request and read a fund's prospectus *before* you invest. The prospectus is the fund's selling document and contains valuable information, such as the fund's investment objectives or goals, principal strategies for achieving those goals, principal risks of investing in the fund, fees and expenses, and past performance. The prospectus also identifies the fund's managers and advisers and describes how to purchase and redeem fund shares.

While they may seem daunting at first, mutual fund prospectuses contain a treasure trove of valuable information. The SEC requires funds to include specific categories of information in their prospectuses and to present key data (such as fees and past performance) in a standard format so that investors can more easily compare different funds.

Here's some of what you'll find in mutual fund prospectuses:

- **Date of Issue**—The date of the prospectus should appear on the front cover. Mutual funds must update their prospectuses at least once a year, so always check to make sure you're looking at the most recent version.

- **Risk/Return Bar Chart and Table**—Near the front of the prospectus, right after the fund's narrative description of its investment objectives or goals, strategies, and risks, you'll find a *bar chart* showing the fund's annual total returns for each of the last 10 years (or for the life of the fund if it is less than 10 years old). All funds that have had annual returns for at least one calendar year must include this chart.

Except in limited circumstances, funds also must include a table that sets forth returns—both before and after taxes—for the past 1-, 5-, and 10-year periods. The table will also include the returns of an appropriate broad-based index for comparison purposes. Here's what the table will look like:

	1-YEAR	5-YEAR (OR LIFE OF FUND)	10-YEAR (OR LIFE OF FUND)
Return before taxes	—%	—%	—%
Return after taxes on distributions	—%	—%	—%
Return after taxes on distributions and sale of fund shares	—%	—%	—%
Index (reflects no deductions for fees, expenses, or taxes)	—%	—%	—%

Note: Be sure to read any footnotes or accompanying explanations to make sure that you fully understand the data the fund provides in the bar chart and table. Also, bear in mind that the bar chart and table for a multiple-class fund (that offers more than one class of fund shares in the prospectus) will typically show performance data and returns for *only one* class.

- **Fee Table**—Following the performance bar chart and annual returns table, you'll find a table that describes the fund's fees and expenses. These include the shareholder fees and annual fund operating expenses described in greater detail (on pages 12-14). The fee table includes an example that will help you compare costs among different funds by showing you the costs associated with investing a hypothetical $10,000 over a 1-, 3-, 5-, and 10-year period.

- **Financial Highlights**—This section, which generally appears towards the back of the prospectus, contains audited data concerning the fund's financial performance for each of the past 5 years.

Here you'll find net asset values (for both the beginning and end of each period), total returns, and various ratios, including the ratio of expenses to average net assets, the ratio of net income to average net assets, and the portfolio turnover rate.

Profile

Some mutual funds also furnish investors with a "profile," which summarizes key information contained in the fund's prospectus, such as the fund's investment objectives, principal investment strategies, principal risks, performance, fees and expenses, after-tax returns, identity of the fund's investment adviser, investment requirements, and other information.

Statement of Additional Information ("SAI")

Also known as "Part B" of the registration statement, the SAI explains a fund's operations in greater detail than the prospectus—including the fund's financial statements and details about the history of the fund, fund policies on borrowing and concentration, the identity of officers, directors, and persons who control the fund, investment advisory and other services, brokerage commissions, tax matters, and performance such as yield and average annual total return information. If you ask, the fund must send you an SAI. The back cover of the fund's prospectus should contain information on how to obtain the SAI.

Shareholder Reports

A mutual fund also must provide shareholders with annual and semi-annual reports within 60 days after the end of the fund's fiscal year and 60 days after the fund's fiscal mid-year. These reports contain a variety of updated financial information, a list of the fund's portfolio securities, and other information. The information in the shareholder reports will be current as of the date of the particular report (that is, the last day of the fund's fiscal year for the annual report, and the last day of the fund's fiscal mid-year for the semi-annual report).

Investors can obtain all of these documents by:

- ☑ Calling or writing to the fund (all mutual funds have toll-free telephone numbers);

- ☑ Visiting the fund's website;

- ☑ Contacting a broker that sells the fund's shares;

- ☑ Searching the SEC's EDGAR database at **http://www.sec.gov/ edgar.shtml** and downloading the documents for free; or

- ☑ Contacting the SEC's Office of Investor Education and Advocacy by telephone at (202) 551-8090, by fax at (202) 772-9295, or by email at publicinfo@sec.gov. Please be aware that we charge a per page fee for photocopying.

PAST PERFORMANCE

A fund's past performance is not as important as you might think. Advertisements, rankings, and ratings often emphasize how well a fund has performed in the past. But studies show that the future is often different. This year's "number one" fund can easily become next year's below average fund.

Be sure to find out how long the fund has been in existence. Newly created or small funds sometimes have excellent short-term performance records. Because these funds may invest in only a small number of stocks, a few successful stocks can have a large impact on their performance. But as these funds grow larger and increase the number of stocks they own, each stock has less impact on performance. This may make it more difficult to sustain initial results.

While past performance does not necessarily predict future returns, it *can* tell you how volatile (or stable) a fund has been over a period of time. Generally, the more volatile a fund, the higher the investment risk. If you'll need your money to meet a financial goal in the near-term, you probably can't afford the risk of investing in a fund with a volatile history because you will not have enough time to ride out any declines in the stock market.

LOOKING BEYOND A FUND'S NAME

Don't assume that a fund called the "XYZ Stock Fund" invests only in stocks or that the "Martian High-Yield Fund" invests **only** in the securities of companies headquartered on the planet Mars. The SEC requires that any mutual fund with a name suggesting that it focuses on a particular type of investment must invest at least 80% of its assets in the type of investment suggested by its name. But funds can still invest up to one-fifth of their holdings in other types of securities—including securities that you might consider too risky or perhaps not aggressive enough.

BANK PRODUCTS VERSUS MUTUAL FUNDS

Many banks now sell mutual funds, some of which carry the bank's name. But mutual funds sold in banks, including money market funds, are *not* bank deposits. As a result, they are *not* federally insured by the Federal Deposit Insurance Corporation (FDIC).

MONEY MARKET MATTERS

Don't confuse a "money market fund" with a "money market deposit account." The names are similar, but they are completely different:

- A money market fund is a type of mutual fund. It is *not* guaranteed or FDIC insured. When you buy shares in a money market fund, you should receive a prospectus.

- A money market deposit account *is* a bank deposit. It is guaranteed and FDIC insured. When you deposit money in a money market deposit account, you should receive a Truth in Savings form.

If You Have Problems

If you encounter a problem with your mutual fund, you can send us your complaint using our online complaint form at **www.sec.gov/ complaint.shtml**. You can also reach us by regular mail at:

U.S. Securities and Exchange Commission
Office of Investor Education and Advocacy
100 F Street, NE
Washington, DC 20549-0213
Toll-free: (800) 732-0330
Website: www.investor.gov

For more information about investing wisely and avoiding fraud, please check out the "Investor Information" section of our website at **www.sec.gov/investor.shtml.**

Glossary of Key Mutual Fund Terms

12b-1 Fees—fees paid by the fund out of fund assets to cover the costs of marketing and selling fund shares and sometimes to cover the costs of providing shareholder services. "Distribution fees" include fees to compensate brokers and others who sell fund shares and to pay for advertising, the printing and mailing of prospectuses to new investors, and the printing and mailing of sales literature. "Shareholder Service Fees" are fees paid to persons to respond to investor inquiries and provide investors with information about their investments.

Account Fee—a fee that some funds separately impose on investors for the maintenance of their accounts. For example, accounts below a specified dollar amount may have to pay an account fee.

Back-end Load—a sales charge (also known as a "deferred sales charge") investors pay when they redeem (or sell) mutual fund shares, generally used by the fund to compensate brokers.

Classes—different types of shares issued by a single fund, often referred to as *Class A* shares, *Class B* shares, and so on. Each class invests in the same "pool" (or investment portfolio) of securities and has the same investment objectives and policies. But each class has different shareholder services and/or distribution arrangements with different fees and expenses and therefore different performance results.

Closed-end Fund—a type of investment company that does not continuously offer its shares for sale but instead sells a fixed number of shares at one time (in the initial public offering) which then typically trade on a secondary market, such as the New York Stock Exchange or the Nasdaq Stock Market. Legally known as a "closed-end company."

Contingent Deferred Sales Load—a type of back-end load, the amount of which depends on the length of time the investor held his or her shares. For example, a contingent deferred sales load might be (X)% if an investor holds his or her shares for one year, (X-1)% after two years, and so on until the load reaches zero and goes away completely.

Conversion—a feature some funds offer that allows investors to automatically change from one class to another (typically with lower annual expenses) after a set period of time. The fund's prospectus or profile will state whether a class ever converts to another class.

Deferred Sales Charge—see "back-end load" (above).

Distribution Fees—fees paid out of fund assets to cover expenses for marketing and selling fund shares, including advertising costs, compensation for brokers and others who sell fund shares, and payments for printing and mailing prospectuses to new investors and sales literature prospective investors. Sometimes referred to as "12b-1 fees."

Exchange Fee—a fee that some funds impose on shareholders if they exchange (transfer) to another fund within the same fund group.

Exchange-Traded Funds—a type of an investment company (either an open-end company or UIT) whose objective is to achieve the same return as a particular market index. ETFs differ from traditional open-end companies and UITs, because, pursuant to SEC exemptive orders, shares issued by ETFs trade on a secondary market and are only redeemable from the fund itself in very large blocks (blocks of 50,000 shares for example).

Expense Ratio—the fund's total annual operating expenses (including management fees, distribution (12b-1) fees, and other expenses) expressed as a percentage of average net assets.

Front-end Load—an upfront sales charge investors pay when they purchase fund shares, generally used by the fund to compensate brokers. A front-end load reduces the amount available to purchase fund shares.

Index Fund—describes a type of mutual fund or Unit Investment Trust (UIT) whose investment objective typically is to achieve the same return as a particular market index, such as the S&P 500 Composite Stock Price Index, the Russell 2000 Index, or the Wilshire 5000 Total Market Index.

Investment Adviser—generally, a person or entity who receives compensation for giving individually tailored advice to a specific person on investing in stocks, bonds, or mutual funds. Some investment advisers also manage portfolios of securities, including mutual funds.

Investment Company—a company (corporation, business trust, partnership, or limited liability company) that issues securities and is primarily engaged in the business of investing in securities. The three basic types of investment companies are mutual funds, closed-end funds, and unit investment trusts.

Load—see "Sales Charge."

Management Fee—fee paid out of fund assets to the fund's investment adviser for investment portfolio management, any other management fees payable to the fund's investment adviser or its affiliates, and any administrative fee payable to the investment adviser that are not included in the "Other Expenses" category. A fund's management fees appears as a category under "Annual Fund Operating Expenses" in the Fee Table.

Market Index—a measurement of the performance of a specific "basket" of stocks considered to represent a particular market or sector of the U. S. stock market or the economy. For example, the Dow Jones Industrial Average (DJIA) is an index of 30 "blue chip" U. S. stocks of industrial companies (excluding transportation and utility companies).

Mutual Fund—the common name for an open-end investment company. Like other types of investment companies, mutual funds pool money from many investors and invest the money in stocks, bonds, short-term money-market instruments, or other securities. Mutual funds issue redeemable shares that investors purchase directly from the fund (or through a broker for the fund) instead of purchasing from investors on a secondary market.

NAV (Net Asset Value)—the value of the fund's assets minus its liabilities. SEC rules require funds to calculate the NAV at least once daily. To calculate the NAV per share, simply subtract the fund's liabilities from its assets and then divide the result by the number of shares outstanding.

No-load Fund—a fund that does not charge any type of sales load. But not every type of shareholder fee is a "sales load," and a no-load fund may charge fees that are not sales loads. No-load funds also charge operating expenses.

Open-end Company—the legal name for a mutual fund. An open-end company is a type of investment company.

Operating Expenses—the costs a fund incurs in connection with running the fund, including management fees, distribution (12b-1) fees, and other expenses.

Portfolio—an individual's or entity's combined holdings of stocks, bonds, or other securities and assets.

Profile—summarizes key information about a mutual fund's costs, investment objectives, risks, and performance. Although every mutual fund has a prospectus, not every mutual fund has a profile.

Prospectus—describes the mutual fund to prospective investors. Every mutual fund has a prospectus. The prospectus contains information about the mutual fund's costs, investment objectives, risks, and performance. You can get a prospectus from the mutual fund company (through its website or by phone or mail). Your financial professional or broker can also provide you with a copy.

Purchase Fee—a shareholder fee that some funds charge when investors purchase mutual fund shares. Not the same as (and may be in addition to) a front-end load.

Redemption Fee—a shareholder fee that some funds charge when investors redeem (or sell) mutual fund shares. Redemption fees (which must be paid to the fund) are not the same as (and may be in addition to) a back-end load (which is typically paid to a broker). The SEC generally limits redemption fees to 2%.

Sales Charge (or "Load")—the amount that investors pay when they purchase (front-end load) or redeem (back-end load) shares in a mutual fund, similar to a commission. The SEC's rules do not limit the size of sales load a fund may charge, but FINRA's rules state that mutual fund sales loads cannot exceed 8.5% and must be even lower depending on other fees and charges assessed.

Shareholder Service Fees—fees paid to persons to respond to investor inquiries and provide investors with information about their investments. See also "12b-1 fees."

Statement of Additional Information (SAI)—conveys information about an open-or closed-end fund that is not necessarily needed by investors to make an informed investment decision, but that some investors find useful. Although funds are not required to provide investors with the SAI, they must give investors the SAI upon request and without charge. Also known as "Part B" of the fund's registration statement.

Total Annual Fund Operating Expense—the total of a fund's annual fund operating expenses, expressed as a percentage of the fund's average net assets. You'll find the total in the fund's fee table in the prospectus.

Unit Investment Trust (UIT)—a type of investment company that typically makes a one-time "public offering" of only a specific, fixed number of units. A UIT will terminate and dissolve on a date established when the UIT is created (although some may terminate more than fifty years after they are created). UITs do not actively trade their investment portfolios.

SEC

OFFICE *of* INVESTOR
EDUCATION *and* ADVOCACY

1-800-732-0330
www.investor.gov

SEC Pub. 002 (08/07)